the SCIENCE *library*

GREAT SCIENTISTS

John Farndon
Consultant: Richard Tames

Miles Kelly
PUBLISHING

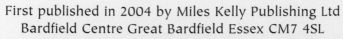

First published in 2004 by Miles Kelly Publishing Ltd
Bardfield Centre Great Bardfield Essex CM7 4SL

Copyright © 2004 Miles Kelly Publishing Ltd

This edition printed in 2008

2 4 6 8 10 9 7 5 3

British Library Cataloguing-in-Publication Data
A catalogue record for this book is available from the British Library

Editorial Director Belinda Gallagher

Art Director Jo Brewer

Editor Jenni Rainford

Editorial Assistant Chloe Schroeter

Cover Design Simon Lee

Design Concept Debbie Meekcoms

Design Stonecastle Graphics

Consultant Richard Tames

Indexer Hilary Bird

Reprographics Stephan Davis, Ian Paulyn

Production Manager Elizabeth Brunwin

ISBN 978-1-84236-988-3

Printed in China

www.mileskelly.net
info@mileskelly.net

www.factsforprojects.com

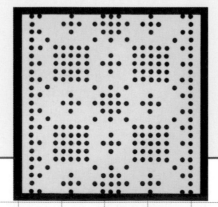

Contents

How to use this book

GREAT SCIENTISTS is packed with information, colour photos, diagrams, illustrations and features to help you learn more about science. Do you know how Hipparchus plotted the stars or how Newton discovered gravity? Did you know who unravelled the mystery of DNA or who split the atom? Enter the fascinating world of science and learn about why things happen, where things come from and how things work. Find out how to use this book and start your journey of scientific discovery.

It's a fact
Key statistics and extra facts on each subject provide additional information.

Main text
Each page begins with an introduction to the different subject areas.

The grid
The pages have a background grid. Pictures and captions sit on the grid and have unique co-ordinates. By using the grid references, you can move from page to page and find out more about related topics.

Main image
Each topic is clearly illustrated. Some images are labelled, providing further information.

26

Bright sparks

WE DEPEND on electricity so much today it is hard to imagine a world without it. Yet about 250 years ago almost nothing was known about it. Electricity is one of the basic forces of the universe, and it exists everywhere. Yet people knew it only as a tiny spark made by rubbing amber or glass against silk. In the 1750s, Benjamin Franklin showed that lightning is electric and soon after electricity became a practical reality. Soon scientists made dramatic discoveries about its properties. About 50 years later, Joseph Henry and Michael Faraday discovered how to generate huge quantities of electricity, and our modern electrical world was born.

IT'S A FACT
• In attempts to repeat Franklin's experiment with a kite in a thunderstorm, many scientists were electrocuted – harmed by the force of electricity.

• Michael Faraday's scientific demonstrations were the top shows of the time, attracting enormous audiences.

Flying a kite
There is no more dramatic sign of the presence of natural electricity in the world than lightning. Yet no one realized just what lightning was until the mid-1700s. At that time, scientists were learning how to make big sparks for the first time by rubbing together materials such as glass on sulphur. American statesman and scientist Benjamin Frankl (1706–1790) wondered if lightning consisted of these same sparks. He conducted a experiment that proved tha electricity is produced by lightning. This discovery le the development of the lightning conductor or roc

Read further › electricity
pg27 (d22)

◄ To test his idea, Franklin kite in a thunderstorm, atta metal key to the string on silk thread. Electricity fron lightning flowed down the to the key and made a hu spark. Franklin had prov – but he was lucky to be

The word 'electricity' comes from 'elektron', the Greek word for amber

1   2   3   4   5   6   7   8   9   10   11   12   13   14   15   16   17

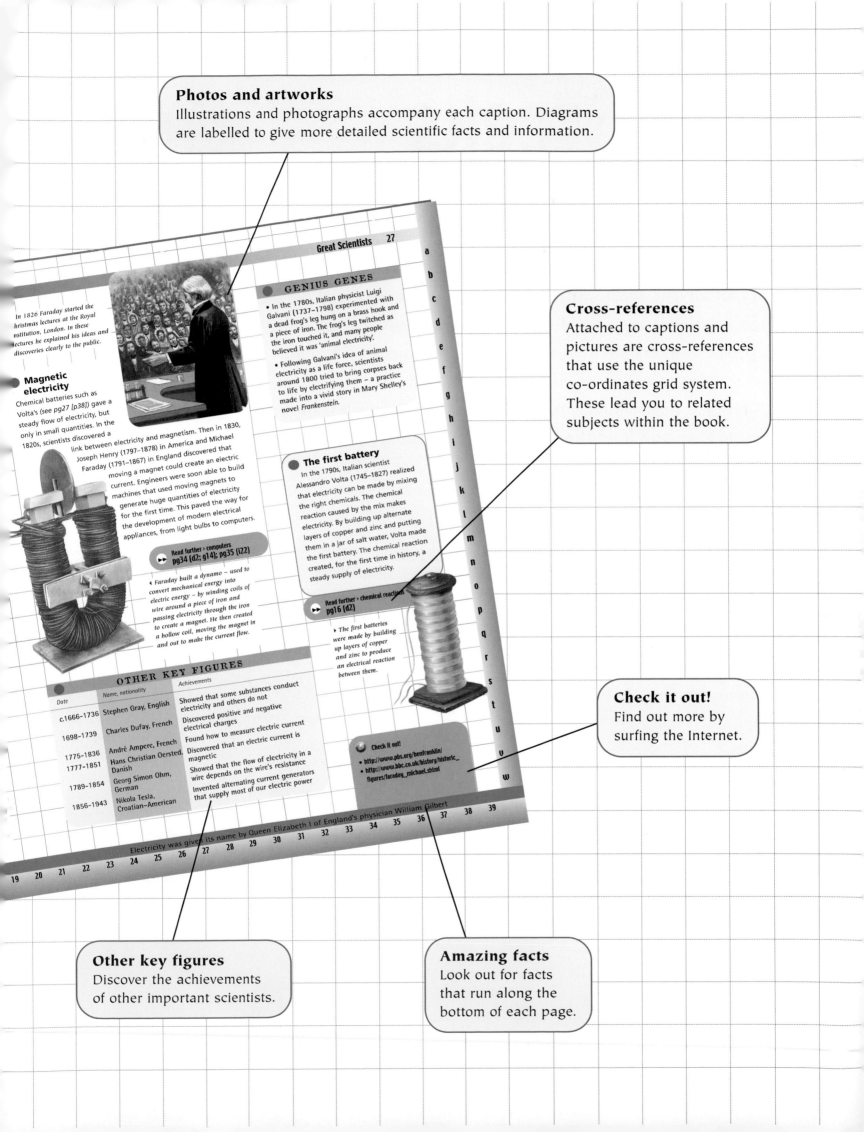

Photos and artworks
Illustrations and photographs accompany each caption. Diagrams are labelled to give more detailed scientific facts and information.

Cross-references
Attached to captions and pictures are cross-references that use the unique co-ordinates grid system. These lead you to related subjects within the book.

Check it out!
Find out more by surfing the Internet.

Other key figures
Discover the achievements of other important scientists.

Amazing facts
Look out for facts that run along the bottom of each page.

Great Scientists 27

In 1826 Faraday started the Christmas lectures at the Royal Institution, London. In these lectures he explained his ideas and discoveries clearly to the public.

● **Magnetic electricity**
Chemical batteries such as Volta's (see pg27 (p38)) gave a steady flow of electricity, but only in small quantities. In the 1820s, scientists discovered a link between electricity and magnetism. Then in 1830, Joseph Henry (1797–1878) in America and Michael Faraday (1791–1867) in England discovered that moving a magnet could create an electric current. Engineers were soon able to build machines that used moving magnets to generate huge quantities of electricity for the first time. This paved the way for the development of modern electrical appliances, from light bulbs to computers.

Read further › computers
pg34 (d2; g14); pg35 (i22)

◄ Faraday built a dynamo – used to convert mechanical energy into electric energy – by winding coils of wire around a piece of iron and passing electricity through the iron to create a magnet. He then created a hollow coil, moving the magnet in and out to make the current flow.

GENIUS GENES
• In the 1780s, Italian physicist Luigi Galvani (1737–1798) experimented with a dead frog's leg hung on a brass hook and a piece of iron. The frog's leg twitched as the iron touched it, and many people believed it was 'animal electricity'.
• Following Galvani's idea of animal electricity as a life force, scientists around 1800 tried to bring corpses back to life by electrifying them – a practice made into a vivid story in Mary Shelley's novel *Frankenstein*.

● **The first battery**
In the 1790s, Italian scientist Alessandro Volta (1745–1827) realized that electricity can be made by mixing the right chemicals. The chemical reaction caused by the mix makes electricity. By building up alternate layers of copper and zinc and putting them in a jar of salt water, Volta made the first battery. The chemical reaction created, for the first time in history, a steady supply of electricity.

Read further › chemical reactions
pg16 (d2)

▶ The first batteries were made by building up layers of copper and zinc to produce an electrical reaction between them.

Check it out!
• http://www.pbs.org/benfranklin/
• http://www.bbc.co.uk/history/historic_figures/faraday_michael.shtml

OTHER KEY FIGURES

Date	Name, nationality	Achievements
c.1666–1736	Stephen Gray, English	Showed that some substances conduct electricity and others do not
1698–1739	Charles Dufay, French	Discovered positive and negative electrical charges
1775–1836	André Ampere, French	Found how to measure electric current
1777–1851	Hans Christian Oersted, Danish	Discovered that an electric current is magnetic
1789–1854	Georg Simon Ohm, German	Showed that the flow of electricity in a wire depends on the wire's resistance
1856–1943	Nikola Tesla, Croatian–American	Invented alternating current generators that supply most of our electric power

a b c d e f g h i j k l m n o p q r s t u v w

Great Greeks

THE NATURAL world was studied by many ancient peoples, but it was in ancient Greece that science really began, in about 2500 BC. Ancient Greek thinkers began to look at the world logically – to work out how natural events occurred by reasoned argument instead of looking for mysterious spiritual forces. Great thinkers such as Plato, Aristotle, Socrates, Euclid and Archimedes made profound insights into the world around them. Their studies included natural forces, mathematics, the nature of matter and how the body works. These studies laid the foundations of modern science.

IT'S A FACT

• The idea that all matter is made from tiny particles called atoms was developed about 2500 years ago by the Greek thinker, Democritus (c.460–c.370 BC).

• The Greek thinker Empedocles (c.494–c.434 BC) divided all matter into four elements – earth, air, fire and water – this idea was not contested until the 17th century.

▼ Archimedes discovered the principle of liquid displacement as he saw the water level in his bath rise as more of his body became immersed. He is said to have jumped out of the bath and run naked through the streets shouting 'Eureka!' – Greek for 'I've got it!'

Ancient scholars

The ancient Greeks called their thinkers and scholars 'philosophers', which means lovers of wisdom. Today we think of philosophy as studies based on thoughts and theories about human existence. But Greek philosophers, often whilst living and studying in Athens, studied all kinds of subjects, including science and mathematics. A temple – the Museion, or Museum – was built in Alexandria in Egypt to celebrate the Greek 'muses' said to inspire ideas and art. The museum had a famous library where scholars from many parts of the world – particularly Greek-speaking countries – came to work.

▼ Greek scholars, such as Plato and Aristotle, developed the idea of intellectual debate.

Eureka!

Greek scientist Archimedes (c.287–c.212 BC) who lived in Syracuse in Sicily (then ruled by the Greeks), was the first to apply mathematics to science. He worked out how effective levers and other machines could be. One of his best ideas was the Archimedean screw, still used today, for pumping water. Archimedes showed that objects float because of the weight of water they displace (push away). This idea is now called Archimedes' Principle.

▶▶ Read further > mathematics
pg24 (d2); pg25 (c22)

▶▶ Read further > House of Wisdom
pg24 (q2)

Check it out!

• http://www.utm.edu/research/iep/a/aristotl.htm

About AD 70, the Greek Hero of Alexander invented a steam engine

1   2   3   4   5   6   7   8   9   10   11   12   13   14   15   16   17   18   19   20

Early medicine

The ancient Greek doctor Hippocrates (460–379 BC) is often called the father of medicine. He lived during a time when many believed that illness was caused by evil spirits or magic. Hippocrates showed that disease has physical causes, such as poor diet or dirt. Today, doctors still practise under an updated version of the 'Hippocratic oath' undertaking to provide good care for their patients.

▸ *Hippocrates recorded people's reactions to certain treatments and so established medicine on a practical basis.*

▶▶ **Read further › medicine**
pg20 [d2; g15]; pg21 [i22]

Covering the angles

Though the ancient Egyptians had a good knowledge of angles and triangles to enable them to build the pyramids, the ancient Greeks created the first systems of geometry – the study of lines and the angles between them. The Greek mathematician Euclid (c.330–260 BC) who studied and lived in Alexandria in Egypt, wrote *Elements of Geometry*, which gave a clear and thorough analysis of geometric principles. Even today, mathematicians refer to the geometry of flat surfaces – lines, points, shapes and solids – as Euclidean geometry.

◂ *Aristotle developed Empedocles' idea of four elements (earth, air, fire and water) into a coherent and logical argument.*

Aristotle

Ancient Greek thinker Aristotle (384–322 BC) studied many areas of science and philosophy at Plato's academy in Athens and helped pioneer the study of animals (zoology) and plants (botany). He established a basic approach to science, showing how scientists must observe things closely, classify these observations, and use logical arguments to understand them. He opened, and directed for 12 years, the Lyceum school in Athens. His ideas remained a key part of university education in Europe for more than 2000 years.

▶▶ **Read further › classification**
pg19 [m22]

▶▶ **Read further › mathematics**
pg24 [g15]

▴ *Classic principles of geometry were put into practice in temples such as the Parthenon in Athens, built between c.447–c.432 BC. It has two adjoining square forms topped with a triangular gable.*

GENIUS GENES

• The Greek geographer Eratosthenes (c.285–c.194 BC) measured the Earth's circumference with astonishing accuracy 1800 years before European explorers showed that the world is round.

• The Greek scholar Xenophanes realized, thousands of years before Victorian scientists developed the idea, that fossils were rocks containing the remains of dead plants and animals.

OTHER KEY FIGURES

Date	Name, nationality	Achievements
c.582–c.497 BC	Pythagoras, Greek	Discovered basic mathematical rules
c.390–c.340 BC	Eudoxus, Greek	Worked out the mathematics of spheres (ball-shapes)
c.265–c.190 BC	Apollonius, Greek	Discovered circles that can be cut from cones, such as parabolas
1st century AD	Hero of Alexandria, Greek	Discovered several uses for steam, such as opening temple doors

Inside the body

FOR 1500 years medicine was based on the writings of Greek physician Claudius Galen (AD *c.*130–*c.*200) who studied animals to support his theories on human medicine. Galen's ideas remained unchallenged until the 15th and 16th centuries when physicians such as Andreas Vesalius and artists such as Leonardo da Vinci began to look at real bodies by dissecting (cutting up) dead human bodies to investigate their structure. This new approach began in Italy at the University of Padua where the great anatomist Vesalius was professor. It spread throughout most of Europe, and later pioneers such as William Harvey and Marcello Malpighi made crucial breakthroughs.

IT'S A FACT

• In the 17th century it was a popular pastime in Italy to watch bodies being dissected in 'anatomy theatres'.

• Physicians used to think illness was caused by an imbalance of one of four natural 'humours' in the body: yellow bile, black bile, phlegm and blood.

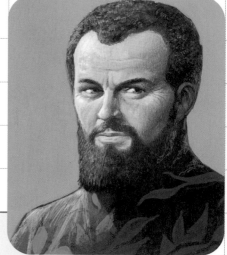

GENIUS GENES

• In the 1820s, Edinburgh medical students needed a lot of bodies to dissect in order to learn about anatomy. So Irishmen William Burke and William Hare began to provide the extra corpses – first by stealing them from graves, then by murdering people!

• When William Harvcy suggested that blood circulated, many people thought he was mad. When he demonstrated blood flowing through a weightlifter's veins, doctor Caspar Hoffman (1572–1648) said, 'I see it, but I don't believe it!'

Knife master

Flemish physician Andreas Vesalius (1514–1564) began the first systematic study of human anatomy – the composition of the human body. Whilst lecturing in surgery at Padua University in Italy, Vesalius saw Galen's books as inaccurate, based as they were on studies of animals. So Vesalius began to carry out his own dissection, though he was not the first. Vesalius dissected the corpses himself, often in front of a large audience of students. His findings were published in *De Humani Corporis Fabrica* – 'On The Structure of the Human Body' – the first great book of anatomy, which was illustrated by Flemish artist Jan van Calcar.

▶▶ Read further › anatomical drawings
pg11 [d22]

▶ *About 30 years before Vesalius, artists such as Italian Raffaello Sanzio (1483–1520) (better known as Raphael) began to observe skeletons to make anatomically accurate drawings of the bones.*

 Check it out!

• http://www.knowitall.org/kidswork/ hospital/history/

The first stethoscope was a paper tube used by Dr René Laennec in 1860 to listen to the heart of a young lady

▶ *Leonardo da Vinci dissected corpses to find out how bodies worked. His drawings were revolutionary in their accuracy.*

Drawing the body

Crucial to our understanding of the human anatomy was the development of accurate anatomical drawings. One of the first great anatomical artists was Italian Leonardo da Vinci (1452–1519). Leonardo had a great mind and contributed to science in countless ways. Human dissection allowed him to produce detailed anatomical drawings to learn how bones and muscles work and how babies grow inside the mother's womb. Accurate drawings enabled physicians to record the results of dissections, and pass on the results to students and other researchers.

▶▶ Read further > recording results pg9 (b22); pg12 (p11)

Body pump

English physician William Harvey (1578–1657) was the first to show that the heart pumps blood. Physicians already knew that blood moved around the body through veins but thought it moved backwards and forwards like tides. Harvey showed that valves in the blood vessels allow blood to continually circulate the body in one direction, flowing from the heart through branching arteries and back through converging veins. However, he could not see how blood moved from arteries to veins.

▶▶ Read further > Malpighi pg11 (n22)

▶ *In describing the circulation of the blood, Harvey labelled veins and arteries to try to understand how blood circulated through the body.*

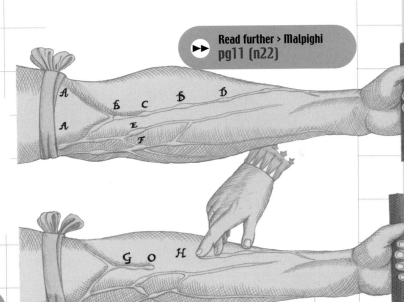

The final link

In 1661, Italian physician Marcello Malpighi (1628–1694) showed how arteries and veins are linked. Using the newly invented microscope, Malpighi saw that arteries and veins are linked by minute blood vessels called capillaries, far too small to see with the naked eye. He also used the microscope to study organs such as the lungs, kidneys, brain and skin.

▶▶ Read further > DNA pg32 (r8); pg33 (p22)

◀ *Microscopes reveal things in the body too small for the eye to see, such as tiny blood cells that float in the blood.*

OTHER KEY FIGURES

Date	Name, nationality	Achievements
c.335–c.280 BC	Herophilus, Greek	Began the science of anatomy
c.304–c.250 BC	Erasistratus, Greek	Began the science of physiology
AD c.130–c.200	Claudius Galen, Greek	Collated all the existing knowledge of medicine and the human body
1523–1562	Gabriello Fallopio, Italian	Discovered tiny structures in the ear and female reproductive system
1561–1636	Sanctorius, Italian	Designed a clinical thermometer and studied the body's metabolism
1809–1885	Friedrich Jacob Henle, German	Discovered kidney tubules
1821–1902	Rudolf Virchow, German	Led our understanding of how disease affects body cells
1868–1943	Karl Landsteiner, Austrian-American	Discovered blood groups

In the 14th century, French soldiers carried spider webs to pack into wounds and stop them bleeding

Star gazers

ASTRONOMY IS one of the oldest sciences. It dates back to the earliest days of humankind when hunters gazed into the night sky to work out which night would give them a full Moon – and more light to hunt by. When people began to form settlements and farm the land, astronomers told farmers when the seasons would come and go. Ancient Egyptians, such as Imhotep, who designed the first pyramid 4500 years ago, were known for their astronomy so it was already an ancient art by the time Greek astronomer Hipparchus began to study the sky.

◄ As well as plotting the position of about 850 stars, Hipparchus invented trigonometry, which is used to mathematically calculate the angles and lengths of the sides of triangles.

● Early star

The ancient Greek astronomer Hipparchus of Rhodes lived during the second century BC. His amazingly accurate observations laid the foundations of astronomy for more than 2000 years. Using the naked eye and astronomical instruments that he had invented himself, Hipparchus plotted the positions of all the stars in the sky visible to the naked eye. He used them to work out the length of one year to within less than seven minutes. He also assigned Magnitudes (a measure of brightness) to all the stars. He called the brightest, the Dog Star Sirius, a First Magnitude star and the faintest he could see, a Sixth Magnitude. Astronomers still use this system today.

►► **Read further › Copernicus**
pg13 (b22)

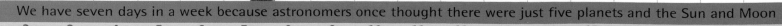
We have seven days in a week because astronomers once thought there were just five planets and the Sun and Moon

| 1 | 2 | 3 | 4 | 5 | 6 | 7 | 8 | 9 | 10 | 11 | 12 | 13 | 14 | 15 | 16 | 17 | 18 | 19 | 20 |

● Moving the Earth

Until the 16th century, most people believed that the Earth was at the centre of the universe, and that the Moon, Sun, planets and stars all revolved around it. But the Polish astronomer Nicolaus Copernicus (1473–1543) thought that the occasional backward loops in the movement of some planets through the sky did not support this theory. From his observations, Copernicus developed the revolutionary new theory that the Sun, not the Earth, was at the centre of the universe. This idea was so shocking that it was more than 100 years before it was widely accepted.

▼ *Copernicus discovered that the Earth and other planets move around the Sun. He also observed that the Earth takes one year (365 days) to travel around the Sun and revolves on its own axis once in every 24-hour period (a day).*

◄ *Copernicus' book, De Revolutionibus orbium coelestium – 'On the Revolutions of the Heavenly Spheres' – published in 1543, was placed on the 'Index', a list of books banned by the Roman Catholic Church, until 1835.*

● Seeing the universe

Less than 100 years ago it was thought that the universe was little bigger than our local Milky Way Galaxy. Then in the 1920s, American astronomer Edwin Hubble (1889–1953) began to study the Andromeda Galaxy. Astronomers had previously thought this was just a cloud of gas called a nebula. But with a very powerful telescope Hubble saw that it was another galaxy full of stars. Soon many other galaxies were discovered and it became clear that the universe is gigantic. In 1927 Hubble made another discovery – that all the galaxies are zooming away from us. He realized that the universe is actually expanding (getting bigger) all the time.

▶▶ **Read further > solar system**
pg25 (b31)

▶▶ **Read further > telescope**
pg15 (b22)

▲ *Hubble showed that the fuzzy patches of light once thought to be nebulae were in fact other galaxies far beyond the milky way.*

OTHER KEY FIGURES

Date	Name, nationality	Achievements
c.2600 BC	Imhotep, Egypt	First known astronomer
270–190 BC	Eratosthenes, Greek, born in Cyrene (now Libya) and lived in Egypt	Made the first accurate measurement of the Earth's circumference
AD 90–170	Ptolemy, Egyptian-Greek	Wrote a guide to astronomy that was the standard textbook for 1400 years
1546–1601	Tycho Brahe, Danish	First to spot an entirely new star
1571–1630	Johannes Kepler, German	Discovered that planets move not in circles but oval-shapes called ellipses
1738–1822 1750–1848	Sir William Herschel, Caroline Herschel, German-British	Worked together to discover the planet Uranus and over 300 different stars

🌑 **Check it out!**

• http://space.about.com/library/weekly/aa103102a.htm

The famous astronomer Tycho Brahe wore a false metal nose, after his real nose was cut off in a duel

Three greats

UNTIL THE 17th century, much of our view of the natural world was based on superstition. Then three of the greatest scientists of all time developed our understanding and perceptions of the world around us. Italian astronomer Galileo Galilei laid the foundations of our understanding of how things move. Englishman Isaac Newton showed that all things move according to three simple rules, and realized that gravity is a force. Dutchman Christiaan Huygens suggested that light travels as waves.

The great Newton

Born in England, Isaac Newton (1642–1727) was one of the greatest scientists. His greatest achievement was his discovery of gravity and three fundamental laws of motion, which he described in his famous book published in 1687, *Philosophiae naturalis principia mathematica* – 'The Mathematical Principles of Natural Philosophy' – usually called just *The Principia*. But he made many other important discoveries, including the fact that white light is a mixture of all colours. He found that by shining it through a prism (wedge of glass), white light could be split into a spectrum – an array of all seven colours. He also invented the mirror telescope to prevent coloured edges on the image. This design is still used in manufacturing many modern telescopes.

Read further > telescopes
pg13 (d33); pg15 (b22)

◀ As Newton showed, a glass wedge or prism bends different colours of light different amounts, so white light is split into all seven colours of the rainbow (red, orange, yellow, green, blue, indigo, violet).

Gravity

Before Newton, no one knew why things fall to the ground or why planets go around the Sun. Newton said that the idea came to him one day while sitting in an orchard. As an apple fell nearby, Newton wondered if the apple was not simply falling but was actually being pulled down by an invisible force. From this simple idea, Newton developed his theory of gravity – a universal force that tries to pull all matter together.

Read further > gravity
pg30 (q12)

Check it out!
- http://www.infoplease.com/ce6/people/A0835490.html
- http://www.imahero.com/hero history/galileo_herohistory.htm

Galileo lived the last years of his life under house arrest – his sentence was not formally withdrawn by the church until 1992

1 2 3 4 5 6 7 8 9 10 11 12 13 14 15 16 17 18 19 20

Yet it does move!

Galileo (1564–1642) helped us to understand how things move, by proving that nothing changes, stops or starts, goes faster or slower unless a force is applied. He also found that if something moves faster, the rate it accelerates at depends on the strength of the force. Galileo also used the newly-invented telescope to discover that Jupiter has four moons and that Venus goes through phases like our Moon. His observations led to the proof that Copernicus *(see pg13 [b28])* was right: that the Earth is not at the centre of the universe and that it does move around the Sun.

Read further › Copernicus
pg13 [b22]

▲ *In 1609, Galileo made his own telescope. It magnified objects up to 30 times, so that he was able to observe the rings of Saturn and see how many stars there were in the solar system. The scholars he showed it to thought that it was a cheat and that he had painted magnified views on the lens.*

▲ *Galileo is said to have muttered 'eppir si muove' – 'yet it does move' – after the Catholic Church, who were so horrified by his theory, made him deny it under threat of torture.*

Light waves

Born to a wealthy Dutch family, Christiaan Huygens (1629–1695) was a brilliant scientist who developed Galileo's idea – of using a swinging weight or pendulum to keep a clock in time – to make the first accurate clocks. Like Galileo, Huygens also made his own telescopes to study the night sky and discovered that vague blurs around the edge of the planet Saturn were actually Saturn's rings. Perhaps his most brilliant insight was the theory that light travels in waves and spreads like ripples when a stone is dropped into water.

◄ *Huygens developed the pendulum clock, which enabled time to be measured accurately.*

Read further › light waves
pg26 [h15]; pg27 [d22]

GENIUS GENES

• Galileo is said to have proved that all objects fall at the same rate, by dropping a wooden ball and a cannon ball from the Leaning Tower of Pisa. In fact it was one of his students who carried out the experiment, because Galileo already knew what the result would be.

• Huygens was the first scientist to write about extraterrestrial (alien) life, in a book called *Cosmotheoros.*

IT'S A FACT

• In 1699, Newton was asked to look after the Royal Mint in England, where coins are made, to try to stop counterfeiting.

• Galileo is said to have got the idea for the pendulum clock by watching a swinging bell rope in the cathedral at Pisa in Italy, the town where he went to university.

a b c d e f g h i j k l m n o p q r s t u v w

Chemical reactions

IN THE Middle Ages, scientists, called alchemists, learned about chemical substances as they searched for a way to turn 'base' (ordinary) metal to gold. Then in 1661, in his book *The Sceptical Chymist*, Irishman Robert Boyle put forward the idea of chemical elements – basic substances that combine to make all other substances. This idea proved to be the founding of chemistry as a science. Over the next 200 years, chemists such as Lavoisier, Priestley, Dalton and Mendeléev applied themselves to discovering these elements and how they worked.

▶ By burning tin inside a sealed container, Lavoisier showed that all substances need oxygen in order to burn.

◀ Robert Boyle was able to speak English, Latin and Greek fluently from the age of eight years.

The burning question

About 250 years ago, most scientists mistakenly believed that flammable materials contained a substance called phlogiston, which dissolved in the air when it burned. The brilliant French chemist Antoine Lavoisier (1743–1794) demonstrated that by burning tin inside a sealed container and weighing it before and after, the tin, far from losing phlogiston to the air, actually gained something. He had discovered the gas that we now know as oxygen. Lavoisier also named many chemicals and arranged them into groups.

▶▶ Read further › compounds pg17 (g32)

▶▶ Read further › classification pg19 (m22)

Robert Boyle

Irish chemist Robert Boyle (1627–1691) developed ideas and experiments that became the basis of modern chemistry. Boyle wrote *The Sceptical Chymist*, which introduced the idea of chemical elements and compounds for the first time, and insisted that ideas should be proven with chemical experiments. Boyle is also remembered for an important physics law – Boyle's law – that shows how the volume of a gas changes if the pressure is changed.

OTHER KEY FIGURES

Date	Name, nationality	Achievements
c.490–c.430 BC	Empedocles, Greek	First to demonstrate that air has no weight
1493–1541	Paracelsus, German	Pioneered the use of chemicals in medicine
1494–1555	Georgius Agricola, German	Developed understanding of metals and minerals
1731–1810	Henry Cavendish, English	Discovered water is a compound of hydrogen and oxygen
1779–1848	Jöns Jacob Berzelius, Swedish	Provided the first list of atomic weights
1838–1907	Sir William Perkin, English	Created the first chemical dye

Dalton kept a journal from the age of 21 to record about 200,000 meteorological (weather) observations

a
b
c
d
e
f
g
h
i
j
k

The true nature of air and water

According to the ancient Greeks, air and water are both fundamental elements, and in the 18th century most scientists still agreed with them. Then in 1774, English chemist Joseph Priestley (1733–1804) discovered a gas that during his experiments made candles burn brightly and allowed mice to breathe. Soon after, Lavoisier experimented with this gas (oxygen) and realized that air is not an element at all but a mixture of at least two gases: oxygen and the gas we now call nitrogen.

◀ *Lavoisier and English scientist Henry Cavendish (1731–1810) discovered that water is not a pure element as the Greeks thought, but a compound of oxygen and the gas hydrogen.*

◀ *If a naked flame is covered and deprived of oxygen, the flame will go out.*

▶▶ **Read further > elements** pg9 (m22)

Elementary table

In the early 1800s, scientists discovered even more chemical elements so that by 1860 more than 60 were known. Yet there seemed to be no order to their properties. Russian chemist Dimitri Mendeléev (1834–1907) arranged them in order of the weight of their atoms, starting with the lightest: hydrogen. He then saw that elements with similar properties could be arranged in eight neat vertical groups. This arrangement, later called the Periodic Table, is now central to our understanding of the elements.

▶▶ **Read further > hydrogen** pg17 (c22)

▶ *Mendeléev showed that you can predict the qualities of any substance, such as hydrogen emitted from power stations, from its place within the Periodic Table.*

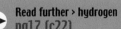

Check it out!

• http://www.infoplease.com/ce6/sci/A0857271.html

GENIUS GENES

• Lavoisier created the first working list of chemical elements in his famous book *Elementary Treatise of Chemistry* (1789).

• When Lavoisier discovered that air is a mixture of oxygen and another gas, he called the other gas 'azote' – Greek for 'no life'. We now call it nitrogen.

Atom man

The idea that all matter is really made of tiny particles called atoms was first suggested by Greek thinker Democritus, 2500 years ago. But English chemist John Dalton (1766–1844) first proved it. He realized that each element is made from atoms of a certain size, and compounds form when atoms of one element join with atoms of another.

▶ *Dalton worked out the weight of each atom by comparing the relative weights of the elements in different samples of different compounds.*

▶▶ **Read further > atoms** pg28 (d2)

q
r

IT'S A FACT

• Joseph Priestley discovered many gases as well as oxygen, including nitrous oxide (laughing gas) and ammonia.

• Priestley left France for England after his house was burned down by a mob angry at his support for the French Revolution. He later moved to the USA to work for the Unitarian Church.

s
t
u
v
w

About 200 years ago, scientists called carbon dioxide 'fixed air'

Evolution

NOWADAYS WE take for granted all kinds of things about the natural world that would have surprised, or even shocked, our ancestors. For example, it was only about 350 years ago, that Dutch scientist Anton van Leeuwenhoek discovered that the world is teeming with many forms of life too small for the naked eye to see. About 200 years ago, naturalists realized that species of living organisms do not always remain the same but, as Charles Darwin showed, they constantly evolve (change) through time. Even the classification of species dates back only 250 years to the discoveries of Swedish naturalist Carolus Linnaeus.

GENIUS GENES

• Linnaeus made reproduction and mating the core of his classification system. He liked to talk of the 'marriage' of plants, with the stamen of the flower, the groom, and the pistil, the bride.

• After each day's teaching, Linnaeus' students would stand around his house shouting 'Long live Linnaeus' – in Latin.

Nature hunters

Our knowledge of the natural world comes from both the work of the great naturalists, and the diligence and interest of countless millions of others – from farmers who learned how to turn wild plants to their own use to early hunters who studied the ways of creatures in order to catch them better. But the twin sciences of botany and zoology were further developed in the 18th and 19th centuries, when naturalists, professional and amateur, began to study plants and animals out of pure interest. Some studied the wildlife just a short walk from home. Others, like Charles Darwin, went all round the world to bring back exotic species from faraway places to study.

▶▶ **Read further › Aristotle and Darwin** pg9 (m22); pg19 (g29)

IT'S A FACT

• In 1683, Dutch scientist Anton van Leeuwenhoek made the first drawing of bacteria – though he had no idea what they were.

• When Linnaeus invented his system, botanists knew of 7700 plants. Now we know of 275,000.

▶ *About 2 million years ago, humans learned how to hunt large animals for food. They chipped flakes off stones to make sharp-edged tools.*

Check it out!

• http://www.aboutdarwin.com/

In Linnaeus' system, most of the names are in Latin

▸ *Hooke invented the compound microscope, which had several lenses. This enabled scientists to see tiny microbes and other living things.*

The tiniest creatures

People never suspected that there were organisms too small for the eye to see – let alone living things – until the microscope was invented around 1590. In the 1670s Dutch scientist Anton van Leeuwenhoek (1632–1723) became fascinated with what could be seen through the microscope. For 50 years he used his home-made, single-lens microscopes to find microscopic creatures in water, which he called 'animalcules', from protozoa to bacteria. In 1665, Englishman Robert Hooke (1635–1703) developed a new version of the microscope to study the form of plants.

▶▶ **Read further › microscopes** pg11 (n22)

Organizing nature

The identification of animals and plants was confusing until Swedish botanist Carolus Linnaeus (1707–1778) devised a system for naming and classifying them all by giving two-part names to every species. The first part is for the genus or group of species with similar characteristics; the second part is its own species name. So every plant and animal had its own name – and its own place in the overall scheme.

◂ Capsella (*genus*) bursa-pastoris (*species*).

OTHER KEY FIGURES

Date	Name, nationality	Achievements
c.372–c.287 BC	Theophrastus, Greek	Father of botany
AD 1665–1721	Rudolf Camerarius, German	Showed how plants reproduce sexually
1823–1913	Alfred Wallace, English	Developed theory of evolution
1825–1895	Thomas Huxley, English	Established humankind's link to other mammals

Life-changing

▶▶ **Read further › Church** pg13 (b22); pg15 (b22)

By 1837 naturalists realized that many extinct species, such as dinosaurs, had lived in the past. By studying creatures on his worldwide voyage aboard the HMS *Beagle*, English scientist Charles Darwin (1809–1882) developed the theory of natural selection. This showed that creatures are all born slightly different; those with a natural advantage, such as being suited to their environment, are more likely to survive and pass on their advantage to their offspring. Darwin showed that some species evolve while some weaker species cannot and so die out. Darwin published these findings in his book *The Origin of Species* in 1859 but it caused uproar because it contradicted the Bible about the origin of human life on Earth.

▾ *Discoveries of bones have shown how our ancestors evolved over millions of years, learning to walk upright, to use tools and eventually light fires.*

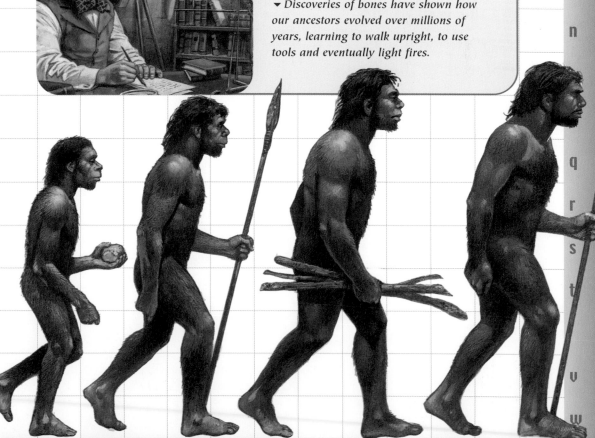

Medical matters

● **IT'S A FACT**

• In 1945, Fleming, Florey and Chain shared a Nobel Prize for their work developing antibiotics.

• The antibiotic streptomycin – the first effective drug against tuberculosis – was discovered in soil fungi by American Selman Waksman (1888–1973).

DISEASE AND ill-health were not always understood and so were often untreatable. People died younger on average than they do today. In the 11th century, Persian doctor Avicenna wrote the *Canon of Medicine*, a medical textbook used across the Arab Empire for centuries. In the late 18th century, Englishman Edward Jenner found a way to protect people against some diseases by a vaccine – a small, harmless dose of the disease, often given by injection. Pasteur's realization in the 1860s that germs caused disease was a huge medical breakthrough, opening the way to the discovery of medicines, such as antibiotics in the 1920s.

● **Persian medicine**
About a thousand years ago, Muslim physicians began to closely study the work of the ancient Greeks such as Hippocrates and Aristotle in order to develop many new ideas on medicine. Persian doctor Avicenna or Ibn Sina (980–1037) worked for Persian rulers and wrote more than 200 books on many subjects, including *Canon of Medicine* which became the standard medical textbook for centuries.

▶▶ Read further › Hippocrates / Aristotle pg9 (b22; m22)

▲ *Avicenna's book* Canon of Medicine *was based in part on the ideas of Aristotle and Galen about how the body works and included information on anatomy and his observations as a doctor.*

● **Antiseptic spray**
English surgeon Joseph Lister (1827–1912) was appalled at the number of deaths caused by infection after surgery. After reading of Pasteur's discovery that bacteria can be air-born, he developed the carbolic steam spray. This produced a fine mist of mild carbolic acid in the operating room, which killed bacteria thus reducing the risk of infection.

▶▶ Read further › bacteria pg21 (b33)

▶ *By using carbolic steam spray, the death rate among Lister's patients fell from 50 to 5 per cent.*

● Check it out!
• http://www.dimdima.com/ science/science_common/show _science.asp?q_aid=165&q_title =joseph+lister

● **GENIUS GENES**

• Pasteur famously exclaimed *'Tout est trouvé!'* ('All is found!') when he discovered isomers – mirror image chemicals.

• When we accidentally say a wrong word that reveals our true desires, it is known as a 'Freudian slip', because Freud suggested it was our unconscious mind that caused the mistake.

OTHER KEY FIGURES

Date	Name, nationality	Achievements
936–1013	Albucasis (Al-Zahrawi), Spanish Arab	Compiled a 1500-page surgical encyclopedia and described 200 surgical instruments
1749–1823	Edward Jenner, English	Discovered a vaccine for smallpox
1813–1878	Claude Bernard, French	Discovered how sugars give the body energy
1843–1910	Robert Koch, German	Proved germs cause disease
1854–1915	Paul Ehrlich, German	Developed chemical drugs for diseases
1881–1955	Alexander Fleming, Scottish	Developed a mould – Penicillin *notatum* – that kills bacteria
1898–1968 1906–1979	Howard Florey, Australian Ernst Chain, German	Worked together to develop the first antibiotic, penicillin

The germ of an idea

French scientist Louis Pasteur (1822–1895) discovered that liquids turn sour because they contain tiny organisms. He found that these organisms can be killed by heat in a process now known as 'pasteurization' whereby a substance, such as milk, is heated to a certain temperature then rapidly cooled. Pasteur's greatest breakthrough was to find that germs, such as bacteria and viruses, carry disease from one person to another. He showed how vaccination works by using a tiny amount of the germ to build up the body's defences.

◀ *Pasteur discovered a vaccine for cattle and sheep against anthrax, as well as a life-saving cure for rabies.*

Thoughts and feelings

Few scientists have had such an impact on our way of thinking about ourselves as Austrian psychologist Sigmund Freud (1856–1939). Freud suggested that we have 'conscious' thoughts, which we know about, and 'unconscious' thoughts, which we do not – but which both influence our behaviour. Freud believed that our childhood experiences play an important role in shaping our unconscious thoughts and that our behaviour as adults is affected by these thoughts.

▶ *Freud believed in talking to his patients about their problems to find out if any past experiences in their lives affected their behaviour as adults.*

Read further › Freudian slips pg20 (s14)

Read further › bacteria pg20 (p2)

Rocks and plates

ROCKS ARE the oldest things on Earth, yet geology – the study of rocks – is a fairly new science. Although Arab scholars such as Avicenna had studied rocks in the 11th century, most people in the West thought that the Earth was just a few thousand years old. Then in the 18th century, people began to wonder if the world was actually much older, and began to study rocks to find out about the formation of the Earth. Soon it became clear that the Earth's long and complex history of formation can be understood by studying rocks.

► Read further > rocks
pg23 (d22)

◄ Many rocks are formed in layers – and geologists can read the history of their formation in the arrangement of the layers.

● IT'S A FACT

• When German climatoligist Alfred Wegener first presented his idea of continental drift in America, one leading scientist said the idea was 'Utter, damned rot!'

• In 1650, Archbishop James Ussher worked out the age of the Earth from the Bible. He decided the world had been formed on Sunday, October 23, 4004 BC.

● GENIUS GENES

• In the 1780s French mathematician, Georges-Louis Leclerc Comte de Buffon timed how long white-hot metal balls took to cool, and estimated that the Earth must be at least 75,000 years old. However, the Earth cools at a slower rate as it is kept warm by interior nuclear processes and so is much older. Scientists now believe that the Earth is in fact approximately 4.5 billion years old.

• Many fossils of identical animals and plants are found in both Africa and South America. Geologists used to think this was because there were once long land bridges between the two continents. We now know it was because these continents were once joined.

● Layer upon layer

We now know that the history of the Earth is 'written' in layers of rock, but this was not always so. A few centuries ago, most people believed rocks and hills owed their shape entirely to the biblical deluge and flood. In the 17th century, Danish geologist Nicolas Steno (1638–1686) realized that layers of rock were originally formed in flat layers, one on top of the other – so the oldest are always at the bottom, even if they have been tilted, twisted and broken since they were formed. This key insight underpins all geology today.

◀ Smith realized that planning canal routes required an in-depth knowledge of the rocks through which the canals would be built.

Rocky routes

Most early geologists did not look at actual rocks. Instead, they read the Bible or studied the ancient Greeks to understand how the Earth was formed. In the late 18th century, Scottish geologist James Hutton (1726–1797) began to study rocks, and engineers building the canals of the Industrial Revolution, such as Englishman William Smith (1769–1839), began to learn about rocks in order to plan routes. Scottish geologist Sir Charles Lyell (1797–1875) used this knowledge to write *Principles of Geology* in1830. Lyell's book firmly established the idea that the world's landscapes were shaped gradually over time, building up layer upon layer of sedimentary rock through the ages. His book remained the geologist's 'bible' for more than a century.

▶▶ **Read further › ancient Greeks** pg8 (d2)

Growing oceans

In the 1960s, American geologist Harry Hess (1906–1969) made a startling suggestion after studying the mid-ocean ridges – the long ridges on the seabed that wind through the middle of many oceans. Hess' idea was that ocean floors are spreading wider from the mid-ocean ridge. As hot rock wells up from the Earth's interior to form the ridge, it pushes the two halves of the ocean apart. Proof of this theory endorsed Wegener's idea of continental drift: that continents do move, and it is the spreading of the oceans that makes them move.

▶▶ **Read further › Wegener** pg23 (m22)

Mid-ocean ridge

Seabed

▲ Ridges down the middle of the ocean floor are created by magma welling up through the Earth's crust, making the sea floor grow gradually wider.

Moving continents

As long ago as the 17th century, English politician and writer Francis Bacon (1561–1626) noticed how well the coasts of South America and Africa match. About 80 years ago, German meteorologist Alfred Wegener (1880–1930) became convinced that these continents match because they were once joined together. He believed that the world's continents are not fixed in one place but drift around slowly over the Earth's surface. However, few people took Wegener's idea of continental drift seriously because they could not imagine how the continents could physically move.

▶▶ **Read further › Wegener** pg22 (c15)

North America

Eurasia (Europe and Asia)

South America

Africa

India

▶ 100 million years ago, North America was still joined to Eurasia, and India was a large island.

OTHER KEY FIGURES

Date	Name, nationality	Achievements
979–1037	Avicenna, Persian	Wrote in his *Book of Minerals* how rivers eroded valleys and layers of rock formed
1785–1873	Adam Sedgwick, English	Pinned down the idea of bedding planes, the boundaries between rock layers

🌐 **Check it out!**
- http://www.infoplease.com/ce6/ sci/A0858359.html
- http://kids.earth.nasa.gov/ archive/pangaea/evidence.html

Wegener died on a journey to the Arctic in 1930, still widely ridiculed for his scientific theories

a b c d e f g h i j k l m n o p q r s t u v w

Maths masters

THE FIRST mathematics was undertaken entirely for practical purposes. Early tax officials – people who collect money for the government – helped develop arithmetic as they worked out tax sums. Ancient Sumerians and Egyptians developed geometry to help build the pyramids and other buildings. Gradually, people became interested in the theory of mathematics and many of the great mathematicians through the ages worked on theoretical problems. The achievements of these theorists were less well known than the work of other scientists, as few people could realise the uses of mathematics.

IT'S A FACT

• Co-ordinate geometry is also known as Cartesian geometry, named after Descartes.

• Al-Khwarizmi said, 'When I consider what people generally want in calculating, I find that it is always a number'.

Pythagoras
Greek mathematician Pythagoras (c.582–497 BC) developed a mathematical rule regarding the lengths of the sides of triangles. This rule, called Pythagoras' theorem, states that the square of the lengths of the two shorter sides of any right-angled triangle add up to the square of the length of the longest side.

▶▶ Read further › geometry
pg9 (b34)

Mathematical letters
Algebra is a branch of mathematics that solves problems by substituting letters and other symbols for different quantities. The name comes from the Latin name for the book where it was first properly described – *Al-jabr* – the full name meaning 'The Compendious Book on Calculation by Completion [or Restoring] and Balancing'. This is one of the most famous mathematics books of all time, written by Arabic mathematician Al-Khwarizmi in about 830.

▲ Al-Khwarizmi taught algebra in the House of Wisdom – a mathematical school in Baghdad (now in Iraq). He wrote his influential book on algebra between 813 and 833.

▶▶ Read further › mathematics
pg8 (m15); pg9 (b34)

GENIUS GENES

• In 1796, Laplace suggested 'the attractive force [gravity] of a heavenly body [an object in space] could be so large that light could not flow out of it' nearly 200 years before astronomers showed this was so in black holes.

• Descartes suggested that it made sense to think of our body and mind as entirely separate. Our bodies and senses are solid, material things; but our minds are something entirely different.

Roger Bacon said in the 13th century 'Mathematics is the door and the key to the sciences'

▸ *For more than 2000 years, Euclid's textbook was used in schools to teach children the basics of geometry.*

Muslim scholars

Greek thinkers such as Euclid achieved much in basic mathematics, but more advanced mathematics was mostly developed by Arab scholars. In the 9th century, the caliph (Muslim leader) Al-Ma-mum turned Baghdad (now in Iraq) into a centre of learning. The focus was the Bayt al-Hikma (House of Wisdom). Al-Uqlidisi gave us decimal fractions; Abu'l-Wafa developed the idea of tangents (special angles in right-angled triangles); mathematician and poet, Omar Khayyam made advances in ways to solve complex equations.

▶▶ **Read further > Euclid** pg9 (b34)

Saving the world

French mathematician and astronomer Pierre Laplace (1749–1827) calculated the mathematics of the orbits of the planets and their gravitational pulls in a way that not even Newton had been able to do. In 1773 he showed how one planet would not be thrown off course by the gravity of another as they passed nearby – an effect Newton had feared might lead to the end of the world. Laplace was also the first to suggest that the solar system was created from a cloud of gas.

▸ *Laplace showed how Saturn does not wobble even when Jupiter passes close by.*

▶▶ **Read further > solar system** pg13 (b22)

Graphic answers

French philosopher and mathematician René Descartes (1596–1650) is best known for his ideas on the nature of human existence. He is most famous for arguing that everything should be doubted before being believed, and for stating that proof that he existed was his ability to think. From this came his famous quote, '*Cogito ergo sum*' – 'I think therefore I am'. He also developed a kind of maths called co-ordinate or analytical geometry. This enables scientists and mathematicians to show statistics using lines of geometry on a graph, so that the statistics can be understood easily.

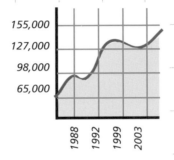

155,000
127,000
98,000
65,000

1988 1992 1999 2003

▲ *Co-ordinate or analytical geometry allows scientists to analyse how fast things change using Cartesian co-ordinates or graphs to plot statistics.*

Accurate reflections

English friar Roger Bacon (1214–1292) made many discoveries in the geometry of reflections from mirrors and the angles of light rays passing through lenses. Bacon also believed that the world was round. This idea was ridiculed and even caused him to be imprisoned.

▶▶ **Read further > light** pg14 (l2)

▾ *Bacon showed that light rays bounce off and hit a mirror at the same angle.*

OTHER KEY FIGURES

Date	Name, nationality	Achievements
c.1170–c.1250	Leonardo Fibonacci, Italian	Introduced the Arabic numeral system we use today in Europe
1561–1630	Henry Briggs, English	Simplified the idea of logarithms
1601–1665	Pierre de Fermat, French	Introduced probability theory and number theory
1707–1783	Leonhard Euler, Swiss	Developed trigonometry
1777–1855	Karl Gauss, German	Developed theory of numbers
1781–1840	Siméon-Denis Poisson, French	Developed probability theory
1854–1912	Jules Poincaré, French	Invented chaos theory

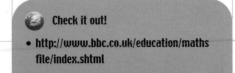

🌐 **Check it out!**

• http://www.bbc.co.uk/education/maths file/index.shtml

Laplace's famous last words are said to have been 'Man follows only phantoms'

Bright sparks

- In attempts to repeat Franklin's experiment with a kite in a thunderstorm, many scientists were electrocuted – harmed by the force of electricity.

- Michael Faraday's scientific demonstrations were the top shows of the time, attracting enormous audiences.

WE DEPEND on electricity so much today it is hard to imagine a world without it. Yet about 250 years ago almost nothing was known about it. Electricity is one of the basic forces of the universe, and it exists everywhere. Yet people knew it only as a tiny spark made by rubbing amber or glass against silk. In the 1750s, Benjamin Franklin showed that lightning is electric and soon after electricity became a practical reality. Soon scientists made dramatic discoveries about its properties. About 50 years later, Joseph Henry and Michael Faraday discovered how to generate huge quantities of electricity, and our modern electrical world was born.

Flying a kite

There is no more dramatic sign of the presence of natural electricity in the world than lightning. Yet no one realized just what lightning was until the mid-1700s. At that time, scientists were learning how to make big sparks for the first time by rubbing together materials such as glass on sulphur. American statesman and scientist Benjamin Franklin (1706–1790) wondered if lightning consisted of these same sparks. He conducted an experiment that proved that electricity is produced by lightning. This discovery led to the development of the lightning conductor or rod.

Read further > electricity
pg27 (d22)

◄ To test his idea, Franklin flew a kite in a thunderstorm, attaching a metal key to the string on a short silk thread. Electricity from the lightning flowed down the wet string to the key and made a huge electrical spark. Franklin had proved his point – but he was lucky to be alive.

▶ *In 1826 Faraday started the Christmas lectures at the Royal Institution, London. In these lectures he explained his ideas and discoveries clearly to the public.*

● Magnetic electricity

Chemical batteries such as Volta's *(see pg27 [p38])* gave a steady flow of electricity, but only in small quantities. In the 1820s, scientists discovered a link between electricity and magnetism. Then in 1830, Joseph Henry (1797–1878) in America and Michael Faraday (1791–1867) in England discovered that moving a magnet could create an electric current. Engineers were soon able to build machines that used moving magnets to generate huge quantities of electricity for the first time. This paved the way for the development of modern electrical appliances, from light bulbs to computers.

Read further › computers
pg34 [d2; g14]; pg35 [i22]

◀ *Faraday built a dynamo – used to convert mechanical energy into electric energy – by winding coils of wire around a piece of iron and passing electricity through the iron to create a magnet. He then created a hollow coil, moving the magnet in and out to make the current flow.*

● GENIUS GENES

• In the 1780s, Italian physicist Luigi Galvani (1737–1798) experimented with a dead frog's leg hung on a brass hook and a piece of iron. The frog's leg twitched as the iron touched it, and many people believed it was 'animal electricity'.

• Following Galvani's idea of animal electricity as a life force, scientists around 1800 tried to bring corpses back to life by electrifying them – a practice made into a vivid story in Mary Shelley's novel *Frankenstein*.

● The first battery

In the 1790s, Italian scientist Alessandro Volta (1745–1827) realized that electricity can be made by mixing the right chemicals. The chemical reaction caused by the mix makes electricity. By building up alternate layers of copper and zinc and putting them in a jar of salt water, Volta made the first battery. The chemical reaction created, for the first time in history, a steady supply of electricity.

Read further › chemical reactions
pg16 [d2]

▶ *The first batteries were made by building up layers of copper and zinc to produce an electrical reaction between them.*

● OTHER KEY FIGURES

Date	Name, nationality	Achievements
c.1666-1736	Stephen Gray, English	Showed that some substances conduct electricity and others do not
1698-1739	Charles Dufay, French	Discovered positive and negative electrical charges
1775-1836	André Ampere, French	Found how to measure electric current
1777-1851	Hans Christian Oersted, Danish	Discovered that an electric current is magnetic
1789-1854	Georg Simon Ohm, German	Showed that the flow of electricity in a wire depends on the wire's resistance
1856-1943	Nikola Tesla, Serbian–American	Invented alternating current generators that supply most of our electric power

● Check it out!

• http://www.pbs.org/benfranklin/
• http://www.bbc.co.uk/history/historic_figures/faraday_michael.shtml

Electricity was given its name by Queen Elizabeth I of England's physician William Gilbert

Atom experts

IN THE first half of the 19th century, it became clear that gravity is not the only invisible force in the universe. Scientists soon began to realize that all matter in the universe is held together by the invisible forces of electricity and magnetism. A string of brilliant scientists, such as James Clerk Maxwell in the 1860s and the Curies in the 1900s, showed that these forces get their energy from atoms – or from the various particles that make up atoms. On the way, scientists learned all about radiation and nuclear power – and atomic bombs.

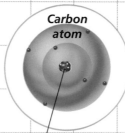

Chlorine atom — Electron
Nucleus with 17 protons

Sodium atom
Nucleus with 11 protons

◄ Atoms are formed with a nucleus at the centre. Each atom has an equal number of electrons and protons. Electrons have a negative electrical charge and move around the nucleus. Protons have a positive electrical charge and cling to the nucleus.

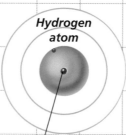

Oxygen atom
Nucleus with 8 protons

Carbon atom
Nucleus with 6 protons

Hydrogen atom
Nucleus with single proton

● Rutherford and Bohr

By the end of the 1800s, scientists knew that everything is made from tiny, invisible bits or 'particles' called atoms. In the 1890s, Englishman J.J. Thomson (1856–1940) showed that there were even smaller particles called electrons. Then New Zealander Ernest Rutherford (1871–1937) showed that an atom is mostly empty space – with a tiny, dense blob at the centre called the nucleus. By the 1930s, Rutherford was working with Danish physicist Niels Bohr (1885–1962) and together they created a picture of the atom – with tiny electrons circling a dense nucleus made from particles called protons and neutrons. We now know that atoms are much more complex, and that there are many particles even smaller than atoms.

►► **Read further › atoms** pg17 (g32)

OTHER KEY FIGURES

Date	Name, nationality	Achievements
1857–1894	Heinrich Hertz, German	Discovered radio waves
1878–1968	Lise Meitner, Austrian	Worked together on the chemistry of radioactivity to discover nuclear fission
1879–1968	Otto Hahn, German	
1902–1980	Fritz Strassman, German	

James Clerk Maxwell made the first ever colour photograph

Fields of force

In the 1840s, the great scientist Michael Faraday suggested the idea of field of force – a region where the effect of an electric current or a magnet is felt. About 20 years later, young Scottish scientist James Clerk Maxwell (1831–1879) showed that these electromagnetic fields spread out or 'radiate' in invisible waves, like ripples around a stone dropped in a pond. He also showed that these waves travel at the speed of light – and deduced that light is in fact an electromagnetic wave.

▶▶ Read further > light waves / Faraday's dynamo
pg15 (n22); pg27 (d22)

▼ Röntgen's X-ray invention allowed doctors to diagnose, for example, lung diseases.

Inside view

German scientist Wilhelm Röntgen (1845–1923) discovered X-rays while experimenting with electron beams. He saw that material glowed while the electron beam was on. This was caused by the X-rays that were produced as the electrons made the material fluorescent. Röntgen received the Nobel Prize for physics in 1901.

Atomic radiation

In 1897 French scientist Henri Becquerel (1852–1908) found that the new kinds of radiation being discovered did not always come from electricity. They seemed to appear around uranium atoms. His work influenced Polish–French scientist Marie Curie who, with her husband Pierre, showed that the radiation was coming directly from the atoms themselves. The Curies called this atomic radiation 'radioactivity'. Tragically, Marie Curie died from blood cancer brought on by her exposure to radioactive substances during her research.

▶ For their research, the Curies, together with Becquerel, won the Nobel Prize for physics in 1903.

▶▶ Read further > radiation
pg31 (i31)

Atomic bomb

Holding the nucleus of atoms together requires an enormous amount of energy. In 1939 scientists split the nuclei of uranium atoms – these are among the biggest and easiest atoms to break. During World War II, American (Italian-born) Enrico Fermi (1901–1954) made particles that flew off, splitting uranium nuclei which then split other atoms. This set off a 'chain-reaction' of splitting that could release huge amounts of nuclear energy.

▲ In 1942, a team under Robert Oppenheimer (1904–1967) in New Mexico used the 'chain reaction' to make the first atomic bomb.

▶▶ Read further > Einstein
pg31 (b22)

🌐 Check it out!
• http://www.chem4kids.com/index.html

Atomic bombs work by splitting atomic nuclei (fission); hydrogen bombs work by joining them (fusion)

Time and space

A CENTURY AGO, our idea of the way the world worked was straightforward. It seemed obvious that things happen, one after another. But two extraordinary scientific ideas – quantum science and relativity – have shown that it is not as simple as that. Quantum science shows that effect does not inevitably follow cause. Relativity overturns our common sense view of time, with time running identically everywhere in the universe. While these ideas have only a limited impact on our everyday lives, they have revolutionized science – from the study of our vast universe to the study of minute atoms.

● OTHER KEY FIGURES

Date	Name, nationality	Achievements
1644–1710	Ole Roemer, Danish	Discovered that the speed of light can be measured
1838–1923	Edward Morley, American	Worked together to show that the speed of light is the same in all directions
1852–1931	Albert Michelson, American	
1902–1984	Paul Dirac, British	Developed quantum physics

● Black holes

Einstein showed that gravity pulls things closer by shrinking the space and time between them. If gravity is incredibly powerful it will shrink space and time to the point where it disappears. In his book *A Brief History of Time*, English physicist Stephen Hawking (born 1942) suggests that this is what happens in the centre of a black hole – a place in space where gravity is so strong that it sucks everything in, including light.

▶ *Hawking's research into black holes, relativity, cosmology and gravitation has gained him numerous scientific awards and honorary degrees. His work provides a strong base for proof that the universe began with a Big Bang, starting from one point and exploding outwards.*

 Check it out!

• http://www.eclipse.net/
~cmmiller/BH/blkmain.html
• http://www.pbs.org/wgbh/
nova/einstein

▶▶ **Read further > Newton and gravity**
pg14 [l2; n13]

If a human fell into a black hole, they would stretch like spaghetti

Everything is relative

It would seem to be the case that time is the same everywhere and moves in only one direction, from past to future. German physicist Albert Einstein (1879–1955) showed that this is not so. In his theory of relativity Einstein completely overturned this idea of time and was the first to show that time is relative. Time is not fixed but depends entirely on how you measure it – and you can only measure it relative to something else. Einstein showed that time does not run one-way, but is a dimension, just like length, breadth and depth, and that it can run backwards as well as forwards.

> ⏵⏵ **Read further › atomic bomb**
> **pg29 (n22)**

◀ Advanced understanding of quantum mechanics has enabled scientists to develop more effective lasers. Because light does not travel in waves but in quanta, lasers focus the light precisely, allowing surgeons to carry out operations, such as removing birthmarks and treating skin disorders.

> ⏵⏵ **Read further › light waves**
> **pg14 (l2); pg15 (n22)**

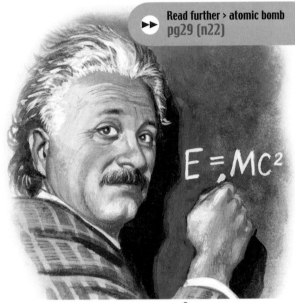

▲ Einstein's equation $E = mc^2$ showed just how much energy there was in an atom, and led to the development of the atom bomb.

Quantum world

Most scientists once thought light and other kinds of radiation travel in waves. But in the 1890s German scientist Max Planck (1858–1947) observed the range of radiation sent out by a hot object – and it did not support the theory that radiation travels in waves. Planck realized that the range of radiation made sense if it was emitted in chunks, or what he called 'quanta'. Quanta are very, very small. When lots are emitted together they appear like smooth waves; when they are emitted separately, they are like particles. Soon scientists realized the quantum concept applied to all kinds of particles smaller than an atom, and quantum mechanics became a whole new science.

GENIUS GENES

• Black holes may be linked by tunnels through space and time called wormholes, to exactly opposite 'white' holes. Wormholes may make it possible to travel through time in the future.

• Teleporting may seem to have come straight from *Star Trek*, but scientists have succeeded in teleporting particles. Using a phenomenon called quantum entanglement, particles are destroyed in one place only to reappear instantly some distance away.

▼ Minkowski used geometry to solve problems in number theory, mathematical physics and the theory of relativity.

Four-dimensional

Hermann Minkowski (1864–1909) developed Einstein's theory of relativity to suggest that space and time were not separate things. Space has three dimensions – up, down and sideways. Minkowski suggested that time was just another dimension. So it made sense to talk of time as the fourth dimension, and join space and time together to create four-dimensional spacetime.

> ⏵⏵ **Read further › geometry**
> **pg9 (b34)**

Quantum mechanics is so complicated that only a handful of scientists in the world understand it

Genetics

DNA's double spiral shape

Each base pairs up with one other base

THE GREAT biologists of the last few centuries have shown us that every living thing is made from thousands or even millions of tiny little packages called cells. Each cell carries with it not only its own instructions for life, but the complete instructions for the whole animal or plant of which it is part. These instructions, called genes, are coded in the structure of a chemical molecule called DNA (deoxyribonucleic acid). DNA works by passing on characteristics from parents to their offspring. Today scientists understand the function of DNA so well that they are beginning to take control of and alter the very materials of life, in what is called genetic engineering.

GENIUS GENES

• Crick and Watson's great discovery of the DNA double helix was based on the work of a young expert in microscopy called Rosalind Franklin (1910–1958).

• Some scientists think they may one day be able to duplicate ancient DNA samples from fossils to make dinosaurs live again, as in the film *Jurassic Park*.

Rungs made from four different chemical bases

◀ DNA is structured in bundles called chromosomes. Humans have 46 chromosomes (23 pairs), which control our characteristics.

Strands of DNA divide to form a template of instruction

IT'S A FACT

• Genetic engineers put fluorescent jellyfish genes in a rabbit, making it glow in the dark.

• In the future, scientists hope to use genetic engineering to make goats deliver spider's web silk in their milk for making ultra-light bullet-proof vests.

▶▶ **Read further › blood cells / vessels** **pg11 (n22; b32)**

The amazing spiral

Even under a powerful microscope, the DNA molecule inside every cell looks like little more than a tangled thread. In fact, its chemical structure is a double 'helix' or spiral – a bit like a twisted rope ladder. The sequence of the 'rungs' is the code that gives the cell instructions by telling it to make particular proteins. When a protein is to be made, the ladder unzips down the middle to expose the code of rungs. Discovering this structure was one of the scientific breakthroughs of the 20th century. It was achieved in 1953 by two young scientists working in Cambridge, England: Englishman Francis Crick (b.1916) and American James Watson (b.1928). Their work won Crick and Watson the 1962 Nobel Prize for medicine.

 Check it out!
• http://gslc.genetics.utah.edu/
• http://www.genecrc.org/site/ ko/index_ko.html

Stitching DNA

One of the greatest scientific discoveries of the 20th century was the idea of genetic engineering or modification (GM). In 1972, American biochemist Paul Berg discovered how to snip a bit of DNA from one bacteria and chemically 'stitch' it into the DNA of another. This achievement, known as recombinant DNA, enables the genes for one characteristic to be moved from one kind of plant or animal into another. Biotechnology firms use this technique to add qualities, such as pest resistance or extra growth, to crops.

OTHER KEY FIGURES

Date	Name, nationality	Achievements
1877–1955	Oswald Avery, Canadian-American	Discovered DNA gave instructions
1905–	Erwin Chargraff, Czech-American	Discovered how DNA bases pair up
1908–1997	Alfred Hershey, American	Developed the idea that DNA gave instructions

DNA plasmid magnified

1. Donor DNA

2. Opened plasmid *Gene*

Bacteria

3. Splicing the gene into the plasmid

4. Bacteria with altered DNA multiplying

Altered DNA plasmid less magnified

Bacteria's ordinary DNA

◀ *This sequence shows the steps in gene splicing. 1. The bit of the donor DNA carrying the right gene is snipped out using restriction enzymes. 2. A special ring of DNA called a plasmid is then broken open. 3. The new gene is spliced into the plasmid, which is sealed up with DNA ligase and introduced into bacteria. 4. The bacteria reproduce.*

▶▶ **Read further › DNA** pg32 (r8)

▶▶ **Read further › offspring** pg19 (g29)

Mendel's peas

The puzzle of how characteristics are passed on from one generation to the next, or even why some characteristics skip a generation, was solved by an Austrian monk called Gregor Mendel (1822–1884). Mendel grew peas, and studied their sizes and colours. By recording how these characteristics were passed on from one generation to the next, he worked out a set of the basic rules of genetic inheritance – how different characteristics are passed down through the generations.

Breaking the code

In 1967 two biochemists: American Marshall Nirenberg (b.1927) and Indian-American Har Khorana (b.1922) broke the genetic code. They showed that the genetic code depends on the sequence of four different chemical 'bases' down each strand of the DNA molecule. These bases are like letters of the alphabet, and the sequence is broken up into 'sentences' called genes. The code in each gene is the cell's instructions to make a protein.

◀ *Identical twins share the same characteristics as each other, caused by their genetic code.*

◀ *Scientists today use the rules of inheritance to determine if diseases are likely to be passed down through generations.*

Genetic engineers hope one day to grow bacteria that will keep teeth clean – for ever

Cyber world

PEOPLE BEGAN to use machines to help them make calculations over 5000 years ago. But the origins of the modern computer date back to the 1830s, when English mathematician Charles Babbage was experimenting with a mechanical calculating machine he called an 'Analytical Engine'. Little came of Babbage's ideas until the invention of electronics about 100 years ago. With the aid of tiny electronic circuits and the invention of the World Wide Web by English scientist Tim Berners-Lee in 1990, computers are now able to do anything from connecting the world via the Internet to producing convincing special effects for films.

The amazing machine

English mathematician Charles Babbage (1791–1871) is sometimes referred to as the 'father of computing'. In 1821 he started work on a machine with rods and gears arranged to compile mathematical tables. He called it the Difference Engine No.1, and it was the first ever automatic calculator.

►► Read further › mathematics
pg24 (d2); pg25 (c22; j22)

Punch cards

Babbage's machine was complete in 1832. At this time he was working on another idea with Ada, Countess of Lovelace. Ada created a punch card program that recorded data for Babbage's machine. This new idea enabled Babbage's machine to perform not just one set mathematical task, but by being 'programmed' with cards punched with holes, to perform any kind of calculation. Babbage called this system the Analytical Engine. Unfortunately, the mechanical systems of the day were not up to the task and it never got built. But the idea of the programmable calculator – the computer – was in place.

►► Read further › mathematics
pg24 (d2)

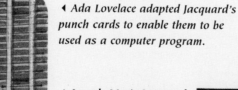

◄ Ada Lovelace adapted Jacquard's punch cards to enable them to be used as a computer program.

▶ Joseph-Marie Jacquard invented the punch card in 1801 to operate his weaving machine. Needles either passed through holes (on) or hit the solid card (off).

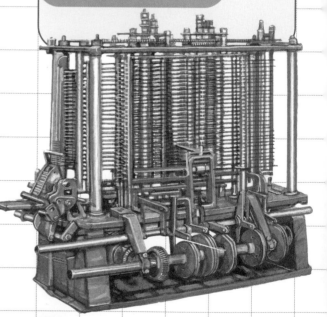

▲ Babbage's Difference Engine was the forerunner of the computer, the first working machine for making mathematical calculations.

◀ *A transistor is the main component built into a computer chip. It controls the flow of electric current, increasing the speed at which a computer can calculate and process information.*

GENIUS GENES

• The microprocessors used in modern computers are collections of linked transistors set in chips of silicon. These are called integrated circuits and were invented by Americans Jack Kilby and Robert Noyce in 1958.

• Babbage said, 'As soon as an Analytical Engine exists, it will necessarily guide the future course of science'.

OTHER KEY FIGURES

Date	Name	Achievements
1623–1662	Blaise Pascal, French	Invented adding machine
1815–1864	George Boole, English	Developed mathematical treatment of logic
1903–1957	John von Neumann, American	Invented first computers with memory

Solid progress

Although computers were built using punch cards in the 1940s, the way forward for computers lay with electronics. But the first electronic computers – like that built by Alan Turing (1912–1954) in England during World War II to crack secret German codes – were built with valves. Valves were electronic switching devices a bit like light bulbs, and a lot were needed to build a computer. Early computers were as large as a room, got very hot, were not very powerful and were always failing. The great breakthrough for computing came when American computer scientists John Bardeen (1908–1991), Walter Brattain (1902–1987) and William Shockley (1910–1989) invented the transistor while working at the Bell Laboratories between 1948 and 1952. Transistors did the same job as valves but they were solid lumps of special material called a semi-conductor. They were the size of a pea, kept cool whilst working and were very robust.

Read further › electricity pg27 (d22)

Check it out!
• http://www.ideafinder.com/history/inventions/transistor.htm
• http://www.greatachievements.org/

Weaving the web

The Internet is now a vast network linking many millions of computers around the world. It began in 1983 with networks that allowed American army computers and university computers to swap data. Then, in 1989, English scientist Tim Berners-Lee (b.1955) who worked at the CERN laboratories in Switzerland invented the World Wide Web. This allows computers to search and find data on any computer that is linked into the Internet. The data you can reach on the Internet is shown on websites compiled of pages of text and pictures. The web makes hyperlinks (fast links) to all the sites containing the search word sent out by a program called a browser.

Read further › early computers pg34 (g14)

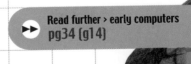

The electronic circuit lines on a modern computer processor are 300 times thinner than a human hair

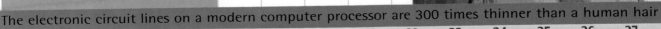

a b c d e f g h i j k l m n o p q r

Glossary

Acceleration When something gets faster or changes direction.

Algebra A branch of mathematics that uses letters to represent numbers when making calculations.

Animalcules The name early scientists gave to microscopic animals.

Antibiotic A medicine, such as penicillin, which works in the body to kill bacteria.

Artery A large blood vessel that carries blood rich in oxygen from the lungs out to the rest of the body from the heart.

Atom The smallest particle of an element.

Atomic bomb A powerful bomb created by splitting or fusing the nuclei of atoms.

Big Bang The idea that the universe formed from a tiny ball about 15 billion years ago.

Black hole A point in space where gravity sucks everything in, including light.

Capillary Tiny blood vessel in the body that links veins to arteries.

Cell The smallest part of a living thing that contains the chemicals of life, such as DNA.

Chain reaction Nuclear reaction that goes on gathering pace by itself.

Circulation The continuous flow of blood around the body.

Combustion When a chemical reacts with oxygen it creates heat, and often light.

Decimal fraction A part of a number shown as if the number was divided by ten.

DNA (Deoxyribonucleic acid) Molecule inside every cell that carries life instructions in the form of a chemical code.

Electron The tiniest particle of an atom.

Element The simplest possible chemical made of one type of unique atom that cannot be broken down.

Evolution The gradual changing of species of living things over time, in response to changing conditions.

Force Something that changes an object's shape or movement by pulling, pushing, stretching or squashing it.

Fossil The remains of a dead plant or animal, usually found in stone.

Fourth dimension Time is the fourth dimension, after length, breadth and height.

Galaxy A giant cluster in space containing millions or even billions of stars.

Gene The life instructions inside every cell.

Genetics The study of genes and DNA.

Geometry The mathematics of lines, angles, curves, surfaces and solid shapes.

Germ A microbe that can cause disease and grow into a new organism.

Gravity The force of attraction between every bit of matter in the universe. Gravity makes everything on Earth fall downwards.

Heredity The passing of characteristics, such as eye colour, through the generations.

Momentum The tendency of a moving object to carry on moving at the same speed and in the same direction.

Natural selection Strong features of living things are naturally selected because those possessing them survive to pass them on.

Nuclear energy Energy released by splitting or fusing the nuclei of atoms.

Nucleus (plural nuclei) The core of an atom, made from protons and neutrons.

Oxygen One of the main gases in the air. It is vital for breathing and combustion.

Particle A tiny piece of matter.

Pasteurization Liquids, such as milk, are heated to a certain temperature and then rapidly cooled in order to destroy germs.

Periodic Table The table of chemical elements arranged in order of the number of protons in the nucleus of their atoms.

Program Coded instructions telling a machine, such as a computer, how to work.

Quantum (plural quanta) A tiny package of light, energy or matter.

Radiation Energy emitted from particles either as electromagnetic waves or as radioactive particles.

Radioactivity The break-up of atomic nucleus, sending out energetic particles that are very dangerous to animal life.

Recombinant DNA The way scientists take DNA from one thing and add it to the DNA of another to alter its life instructions.

Relativity The theory that you can only measure time relative to something else.

Species A particular kind of living thing, such as a lion or an elephant.

Spectrum The range of colours created when light is split by a prism.

Static electricity Electricity that builds up when things rub together. Lightning is static electricity, created when particles in a thundercloud are thrown together.

Theory A carefully thought out idea to explain a particular scientific phenomenon.

Transistor A device made with materials called semiconductors, which conduct electricity using an electric current.

Vaccination A deliberate dose of a mild infection given to build up the body's defences against future serious infections.

Index

Entries in bold refer to main subjects; entries in italics refer to illustrations.